SOUL SONGS OF SUBATHRA

BARNABAS TIBURTIUS
CHRISTY SUBATHRA

INDIA • SINGAPORE • MALAYSIA

ISBN 979-8-89906-625-2

CONTENTS

PREFACE

The book of poems you hold in your hands is a journey through the myriad emotional landscapes that define our humanity. It offers a reflective lens much like the works of the literary greats who have endeavoured to explore the human soul. However, this collection stands unique in its nuanced approach to universal themes, providing readers with a rich tapestry of introspection, empathy, and transformation.

Where T.S. Eliot intricately weaves despair and hope in "The Waste Land," presenting a fragmented world yearning for redemption, this collection's "A Prayer for Restoration" echoes a similar longing for wholeness. Yet, it diverges by offering not just a reflection of despair but a proactive call to action — a plea for compassion and a bridge over the chasm of alienation. Through accessible language that speaks directly to the heart, the poet invites us to embrace empathy, extending beyond the confines of our own sufferings into a realm of shared healing.

In the sphere of self-reflection and resurrection, one might find echoes of Sylvia Plath's introspective depth. Her writings often dive into the personal and the existential, dissecting inner turmoil with a raw precision. Similarly, "An Ode to the Resurrected Soul" explores themes of breaking free from the shadows of cynicism and fear to be reborn with renewed strength. Where Plath's poetry often rests in sombre realisation, this collection finds its uniqueness in offering a beacon of hope — the idea that beyond the confining walls of despair lies the promise of renewal and a light of understanding.

If we look towards the social commentary prevalent in the works of poets like Langston Hughes, who masterfully captured the essence of cultural identity and societal struggle, "Beyond Borders - A Tapestry of Talent" in this collection resonates as a contemporary reflection of similar themes. Addressing the plight and potential of refugees, this poem transcends cultural and geographic boundaries, weaving a narrative of resilience and untapped potential. Through its verses, there is a clarion call for compassion, urging readers to see beyond borders, much as Hughes did through his soulful exploration of racial and cultural landscapes.

The exploration of beauty, both within and beyond the physical realm, can be seen in works akin to John Keats, whose "Ode on a Grecian Urn" delves into eternal beauty. This collection's "Beauty Beyond Appearances" touches on such aesthetic dichotomies, questioning societal norms and perceptions. However, it carves a unique path by emphasising the discovery of beauty not in static perfection, as with the urn, but within the fluid and often chaotic process of life and personal growth.

Rainer Maria Rilke's poetry, particularly his "Letters to a Young Poet," often urges readers to explore their inner worlds, to embrace solitude as a source of insight and creativity. This echoes throughout the introspective passages of poems like "Beyond the Illusionary Mind" in this collection, encouraging readers to transcend superficiality, harnessing the inner voice as a compass to navigate through life's illusions.

The poetical style exhibited in "The Dance of Mind's Evolution" bears semblance to the philosophical inquiries posed by Walt Whitman's "Leaves of Grass," where the exploration of identity and existence takes centre stage. Here, the poet engages with the fluidity of thought and belief, urging change and growth within, mirroring Whitman's celebration of self and the collective human experience yet tailored to our present-day complexities.

In terms of capturing joy and the essence of life's journey, the comparison to Mary Oliver's works, such as "Wild Geese," is inevitable. Oliver's profound observations of nature illuminate her exploration of joy and belonging within the natural order. This is paralleled in "Choosing Joy," a poem from the collection that celebrates conscious joy amid life's adversities, aligning with Oliver's ethos of finding peace and meaning within nature and the ordinary.

However, where Oliver's simplicity often celebrates the natural world as a guide for life's lessons, this collection broadens the lens, intertwining cosmological reflections and universal connectivity beyond the terrestrial. "Stardust to Sapiens," for example, juxtaposes human evolution with cosmic significance, crafting an existential narrative that transcends just the natural realm and delves into our cosmic origins and destiny.

The theme of forgiveness in this collection, explored in "The Alchemy of Forgiveness," invites a narrative reminiscent of Elizabeth Bishop's intricately layered approach to understanding loss and reconciliation, as seen in "One Art." However, what sets this book apart is its commitment to transformation through forgiveness as a tool for emotional liberation, a concept embedded in relational dynamics and essential for healing within both personal and collective contexts.

In conclusion, this collection of poems distinctively captures a multitude of experiences, from personal enlightenment to broader societal reflections, standing at the confluence of grand literary traditions while forging its unique path. It complements the works of established poets, sharing their thematic depth and emotional resonance but distinguishes itself through its modern accessibility and hopeful outlook. Each poem is not merely an echo of past greatness but an exploration of present.

– Barnabas Tiburtius
Chennai

Whose poetry is that you are writing? This haunting question echoes through the corridors of my mind as words, thoughts, emotional outbursts, and ecstatic moments of consciousness pour from my heart onto the page. The essence of these verses is not something I claim as my own; rather, like Khalil Gibran's reflections on children, I view them as words that flow through me, not from me. They emerge from the mysterious depths of the human psyche, echoing the inconsistency and unpredictability that permeate all human thoughts.

Yet, the uncertainty of existence, the whirlwind of questions—who am I, why do I write, is this my destined path or am I overlooking something vital—ignites the stream of introspection, prompting me to continually reassess the purpose and direction of my life. In moments of solitude, I ponder, and my mind, a restless soul, embarks on a journey between extremes, adrift in transitions as feelings agilely guide its course.

These sentiments find voice in my poem, "In the Embrace of Joy and Sorrow":

My mind a restless soul, it seems

Moves between extremes, lost in dreams.

Seeking solace in neither, ever adrift

In motion eternal, by feelings swift.

In these lines, you glimpse the essence of my mindset—a dual existence of joy and sorrow, eternally intertwined, reflecting the profound complexity of the human condition.

This book, a labour of love and introspection, is an anthology of verses born from the echoes of absence. Each poem represents a quest for meaning, a fervent search for what has been lost—a flicker of existence in a vast, mysterious universe. In "Echoes of Absence," I reflect on this eternal search:

I search fervently for what's been lost,

A meaning to existence, a quest.

Smiles that once soothed my soul,

Now dim and fade, leaving me cold.

These lines convey the yearning for moments lost to time, the quest to regain a sense of tranquillity, and the aching awareness of their absence. This introspection is not mere nostalgia; it is a recognition of the subtle, often elusive, truths that emerge through poetic exploration.

When I compose a poem, I devote myself entirely to the present moment, capturing its essence without looking back at previous works. This approach has helped me discover my true self repeatedly, as each poem reflects a distinct facet of my consciousness. My writing is an autobiographical account of thoughts—a poetic diary that chronicles my journey without the constraints or expectations of an audience.

In 2021, as the world came to a standstill amidst a global pandemic, I too heard the anxious thudding of my heart. I questioned whether I had done justice to my existence and if I had adequately embraced the gifts of life. The answer, resounding in silence, was a significant "no." This realization stirred within me an urgency to contribute my voice to the symphony of life's experiences, which had remained dormant for too long.

I embraced writing with fervour, driven by a sense of insecurity and the unknowns ushered in by the pandemic. Yet, this insecurity had nothing to do with what to write, for the words flowed effortlessly. In this endeavour, there existed not why or how, only the when—a response to the call of the present moment.

Through this collection, I share the journey of my introspection, my search for meaning, and my embrace of the poetic flow unhampered by confines of audience or expectation. Each poem stands as a testament to the boundless introspective reach of the human spirit, offering readers glimpses into their own inner landscapes.

My hope is that these verses resonate with you, the reader. May you find reflections of your own thoughts, emotions, and experiences within this collection, as I have found fragments of myself through its creation. In the end, the value of poetry lies in its ability to transcend, to connect disparate human experiences in a tapestry woven with the threads of our shared existence.

As you turn the pages, may you embark on a journey of introspection and discovery, and may the verses inspire you to explore the depths of your own consciousness with an open heart and a curious mind. This book is not merely a collection of poems; it is an invitation to reflect, to question, and to embrace the beauty of uncertainty.

– Christy Subathra

Tiruchirappalli

April 2025

INTRODUCTION

The book of poems you are about to embark upon is a profound journey through the landscape of the human heart, mind, and soul. Each poem is a tapestry of emotions carefully woven with words, offering readers a lens through which to explore the myriad experiences and reflections that comprise our existence. This collection delves into themes of restoration, resurrection, and the human condition, capturing the timeless essence of what it means to live and to feel deeply.

At its core, this anthology serves as a prayer — a yearning for the restoration of compassion, connection, and understanding in an often-fragmented world. The opening poem, "A Prayer for Restoration," sets the stage for this quest, inviting readers to consider their own role in building bridges across the chasms of alienation. With empathy as a beacon, the poet urges a breaking of chains that bind our hearts, allowing for the universal gift of happiness to flourish in shared humanity.

The journey then traverses through moments of introspection and renewal, captured in "An Ode to the Resurrected Soul." Here, the reader is led through a metaphorical labyrinth, where despite the trials and perceived endings, the soul emerges resilient and reborn. This poem, like many others in the collection, reminds us of the relentless forward momentum of life and the strength found in vulnerability and rebirth.

The poems offer a contemplation on the human condition — our aspirations and disillusionments, our joys and our sorrows. "Bearing Our Human Condition" reflects on the passage of time and the wisdom garnered from both the shadows and the light of lived experience. It acknowledges the ebb and flow of life, where our paths converge and diverge, creating a rich tapestry of communal and individual narratives.

"Beauty Beyond Appearances" challenges the superficial judgments that often cloud our perception of self and others. The poem urges an exploration of deeper beauty, untethered from the constraints of societal expectations, and invites a journey into the heart where true grace resides.

As you delve deeper, "Beneath the Veil of Comparison" unravels the corrosive nature of envy and the constant quest for validation. The poet beckons us to embrace our unique strengths and find completion within our own stories, rather than through the accomplishments of others.

The collection is punctuated with calls for guidance and enlightenment; 'Beseeching You to Guide My Path' is a heartfelt plea for divine illumination in times of uncertainty and doubt. The act of seeking becomes a recurrent theme — a desire to transcend beyond the illusionary mind and find solace and truth in a higher consciousness.

In 'Beyond Borders - A Tapestry of Talent,' the poet expands the scope to include a commentary on the plight of refugees, urging a collective awakening to the boundless potential harboured within every soul seeking respite from turmoil.

The exploration of self continues with poems like 'Beyond the Illusionary Mind' and 'Boundless Quest,' which delve into the intricacies of identity, growth, and the pursuit of genuine joy. These reflective pieces encourage readers to transcend personal limitations and societal illusions, embracing a life of fulfilment and authenticity.

A notable highlight, 'Choosing Joy,' offers a contemplative meditation on the power of positive focus amidst life's adversities, inspired by Viktor Frankl's enduring optimism. It champions the resilience of the human spirit in rising above sorrow and finding delight in the simplest of truths.

'Chronicle of Pardon' and 'Churning of the Ocean' navigate the themes of forgiveness and transformation, illustrating the profound impact of letting go and embracing change. These poems resonate with the enduring quest for peace and acceptance amid life's turbulent seas.

As you journey through this book, 'Constant Seeking' and 'A Constant Struggle' further articulate the internal battles waged in the pursuit of serenity and understanding. Each poem serves as a milestone in the broader narrative of personal evolution and enlightenment.

Ultimately, this collection is an homage to the timeless dance between light and shadow, the merging of love and loss, and the enduring quest for truth and beauty. It invites readers to reflect, to understand, and to celebrate the intricate tapestry of human existence.

May these poems inspire introspection, ignite passions, and facilitate a deeper connection with the world within and around us. Each verse is an invitation to pause, to feel, and to find solace in the shared journey of seeking, understanding, and embracing life in all its nuances.

This introduction encapsulates the thematic essence of the poems, setting the stage for a thoughtful and engaging exploration of the collection.

Acknowledgement

Attribution to image from 'STOCKCAKE IMAGES'
Photo by <a href="https://stockcake.com/i/soul-taking-flight_2132676_1374800">Stockcake</a>

A PRAYER FOR RESTORATION

In hesitant moments, my smile begins to form
Ignoring neighbours' woes, I escape the storm
Compassion's shut out; my mind stays cold
Helplessness grips, within my heart takes hold

I recall the chasm, a vast sea of sorrow,
A fleeting stage, a dark tomorrow.
Yet in that abyss, a glimmer did unfold,
A possibility of empathy, a story untold.

Life and way, bestow your grace,
Reveal the truth in every face.
Happiness, a universal gift we share,
Each sadness, a shadow, a burden to bear.

Subjective cleansing, a balm for pain,
Breaking the chains of alienation's disdain.
A lack of concern, a rejection of mind,
Leaving countless sorrows, unattended, confined.

Hands that took life, now cradle a child,
In the same soil, tainted and wild.
Silent contemplation of my existence,
As I grapple with a profound resistance.

A single question echoes, what can I do?
Sinking into depths of reactionless rue.
Calling upon you, the begetter divine,
Resting hope on your shoulders, a lifeline.

In awareness of pain, many experiences arise,
Fear of sinking into darkness, trembling inside.
Grasping your Divine feet with all my might,
Author of creation, shining in your cosmic light.

Resting hope in you, the healer supreme,
Harbinger of fullness, in our collective dream.
A great light to dawn on the near horizon,
Divine restoration, where suffering is unison.

AN ODE TO THE RESURRECTED SOUL

In a labyrinth of phantom walls, I find,
Declaring all is lost, the end in sight,
Yet past them, I hurdle, unconfined,
In the ceaseless race of day and night.

At this juncture, where words feel frail,
And thoughts like echoes futile seem,
I rise like a tree from history's tale,
Resurrected, in life's flowing stream.

With newfound strength, I am born anew,
Gazing upon life's infant strides,
Learning to walk, with skies so blue,
I grasp the truth in changing tides.

No longer shall I cower in fear,
Shield raised against imagined plight,
Life's true essence now becomes clear,
In destruction's dance, in history's light.

Oh, Father, reveal my folly's face,
In clinging to shadows, to empty air,
Guide me to hold what's meant to embrace,
And banish illusions born of despair.

Remind me, O Father, of your decree,
That destiny's thread won't slip away,
Even as smiles fade into pleas,
And souls in weariness find dismay.

With but a word, reshape my view,
Plant the seed of faith, unwavering and true,
That all unfolds as you will it to be,
Resurrecting joy each day in me.

You, my refuge, impregnable and kind,
Granting asylum, compassion's divine,
With love unbounded, my heart entwined,
I praise you, I praise you, for you are mine.

BEARING OUR HUMAN CONDITION

In shadows cast by fleeting years we stand,
Bearing our human condition's weight,
A journey etched by both our heart and hand,
Through trials and triumphs, early and late.

In youth, dreams burn bright, hearts aflame,
Ambition fuels purpose, fierce and bright name.
Yet aging reveals life's shifting clever game,
Aspirations tempered by wisdom's light aim

In sorrow's grasp, we find our deepest soul,
Pain and loss, carve our hearts' deep well,
But in our tears, we also find our role,
To empathize with others, we must dwell

In joy, our spirits soar to heights untold,
Each moment cherished, precious and profound,
In love's warm embrace, we find we're whole,
As human souls in unity are bound.

With every step, our paths converge and part,
The human condition, a tapestry of art,
Through laughter, tears, and every beating heart,
We navigate this journey, play our part.

BEAUTY BEYOND APPEARANCES

More than hunger, more than love's embrace,
A treasure that none can replace,
The image we hold, appearance's grace,
In the human mind, it finds its place.

Above all else, it takes priority,
The impact of illness, the doctor's authority,
I see with concern, the world's dichotomy,
Skin color and beauty, their absurdity.

In the quest for truth beyond what we see,
Traveling nervously, seeking to be free,
From pain and grief, love's sweet decree,
Creation's agitation, a moment's decree.

The mind extends beyond mere illusion,
Roots of autonomy, in a world of confusion,
Seeking beauty, with heartfelt fusion,
In the normalcy of life, a dream's inclusion.

In appearance, we find cracks and divides,
Split moods and pain that ever abides,
Yet in the depths of despair, we decide,
To seek the beauty that lies inside.

Beyond broad and narrow minds, we explore,
In search of results, we seek even more,
The inner light's beauty, at our core,
An endless appearance we can't ignore.

In prayer, we extend love, cosmic in scale,
A big deal, a great thing, our hearts unveil,
For the essence of disaster, we must prevail,
In the beauty of life's journey, we set sail.

BENEATH THE VEIL OF COMPARISON

Comparison and envy, twins entwined,
Their rule upon our hearts defined.
Above me, others' successes shine,
Yet joy eludes, misery is mine.

Smoke rising, stomach churns, a fire's birth,
Envy's flames scorching all worth.
Praise given, yet calculations stir,
Where do I stand in this grand theatre?

Guided by a Lord who sees no smallness,
Yet I'm ensnared in comparison's harness.
Seeking freedom from this lurking vice,
A shadow cast over life's every spice.

"I stand tall," I whisper, trying to deceive,
But the sinking feeling, I cannot leave.
Trapped once more in the mire's embrace,
Comparison's venom, a relentless chase.

I plead for light in this inner strife,
To see strength, beauty, as part of life.
May I embrace the world as my own,
Completing what's lacking, seeds sown.

BESEECHING YOU TO GUIDE MY PATH

With a mind that wanders, unsure what to say,
I find myself stumbling, in disarray,
A chaos of thoughts, a tumultuous shout,
A jumble of words, all tangled about.

My soul is troubled, deep introspection,
A torment of doubt, a painful reflection,
Like water on floor, I flow and I spread,
With no thought for the path I tread.

My actions and thoughts, not truly my own,
A destiny impressed, many ages ago,
A path that is arduous, but I cannot see,
Blinded by the illusion of being free.

Awakening my soul with your radiant light,
To the truth and path that's taken right,
With patience, hope, forgiveness, and light I stride,
Transcending opposites, finding what's right inside.

Your radiant light awakens my soul anew.
To the truth and path that's right, too.
With patience, hope, and forgiveness, I stride.
Transcend opposites, finding what's right inside.

BEYOND BORDERS – A TAPESTRY OF TALENT

In lands where dreams are bound by tears,

Where echoes of despair fill the years,

Refugees in search of a place to belong,

Their cries a haunting, unending song.

From Syria's ruins to Gaza's plight,

Children roam beneath a starless night,

In Lebanon, hope flickers dim and cold,

While the world watches, their story untold.

Rohingya cast from their homes and kin,

Adrift on seas of sorrow, deep within,

Voices unheard amid global din,

Innocent hearts where dreams begin.

Yet in each soul, a spark resides,

A well of talent that still abides,

If only given a chance to rise,

They'd light up the world with untold skies.

Empowered minds, skills refined,

A wealth of culture intertwined,

They knock on doors of affluent lands,
Bearing the gifts of their weary hands.
What if walls turned into open gates,
Compassion's bridge bridging bitter fates,
Imagine the stories yet to unfold,
If courage and kindness took a bold hold.
Innovation thrives where borders cease,
Where harmony and hope increase,
Nations would prosper, rich and new,
For refugees are dreamers too.
The world could share its light and space,
To heal the wounds and embrace each face,
For talent knows no bound or race,
In their eyes, the future's trace.
Listen to their whispered lore,
A testament to what they bore,
In giving them a chance to stand,
We enrich our world, our shared homeland.
With every soul we lift from pain,
We break the silent, binding chain,
In unity, we'd find our gain,
Together, peace and progress sustain.
For talent, once nurtured and restored,

Can soar beyond what was ignored,

A beacon bright, forever forward,

A legacy of love and reward.

Let nations heed this earnest plea,

To see refugees as they might be,

For in their hands, our fate may lie,

A richer world for you and me.

BEYOND THE ILLUSIONARY MIND

In the search for reasons and reactions,

I am lost within my mind's distractions,

Limitations, enslaving holding me back,

From finding true path to what I truly lack.

Intelligence, I thought, was the key,

But it's just an emotion, you see,

A precursor to experience and growth,

An element needs varied paths both.

Feelings can lead us astray,

Generating false destinies along the way,

But love, ah love, that cosmic content,

Opens up my heart's undeniable intent.

Your abundant love, my true mind,
Protects me from false security's bind,
Interplaying with my limited emotion,
Nourishing, enriching with deep devotion.

Grant me the gift of discernment,
To weed out temptations dominant,
Give me strength to surpass all loss and pain,
A never abating desire for your abode to gain.

With your help, I can break free,
From the illusions that hold onto me,
And find the truth, pure and bright,
In your love, my guiding light.

BOUNDLESS QUEST

From void if all did truly spring,
My grasp on what lies deep within,
Is lost, a search with hindered wing.
To call unknown "mere nothingness" is sin.

Growth's lack, a dead end in my quest,
Yet grace reveals the path ahead,
No final articulation in a boundless test,
Realising the inadequacy my knowledge tread.

Love's limit? Wisdom's core unknown?
Beauty's first brushstroke, where's the source?
These endless values, all my own,
One drop can't measure their endless course.

Release the self, false attachments cease,
A timeless journey, wisdom's sacred quest,
All-encompassing inner spark of eternal peace,
Engulf me ocean of knowledge, ever blessed.

CHOOSING JOY

In a world heavy with reasons to be sad,
Choose joy like a child, make hearts glad.
Like crayons paint a vibrant sky above,
Choose joy consciously, fill your heart with love.

At first, it's a struggle, an effort you'll find,
Pressing against sorrow, a weight on the mind.
Restless with action, take steps you must,
Feel sorrow deeply, in life, you'll learn trust.

But keep pressing joy against sorrow's vast sea,
Until it flows freely, like a river running free.
Automated, like gravity's gentle force,
An inner law of nature, a joyful, steady course.

Viktor Frankl exclaimed, "Yes to life!" he cried,
In spite of everything, he chose joy as his guide.
Amid the rubble of our shattered plans so small,
We too can embrace joy, rise above it all.

Joy's not from life's absence of strife,
But function of focus, elevating our life.
A fulcrum of choice through each days,
Thread to weave life's intricate maze.

Delight in the old man, age-salted and wise,
On the street corner, waiting with tender eyes.
His faithful dog by his side, a bond pure and true,
In their subtle devotion, find joy in their view.

Delight in the girl, a graceful vision,
Zooming past on her bike some mission.
Rainbow tassels, a golden helmet bright,
A fierce joy, future's radiant light.

Delight in the snail's slow, deliberate quest,
As it crosses the sidewalk, a tiny, brave guest.
For the taste of one blade of grass, it explores,
A lesson in patience, in joy, it restores.

Delight in the new leaf, tender and green,
Unfurling with grace like a mystical dream.
From the parched stem, it gently springs,
A symbol of hope and nature's joy brings.

Choose joy like a child in moments small,
Let it lift your spirit, seeing spring's call,
Find life's treasures in simple joys bright,
Choose joy daily, hearts echo with delight.

A CHRONICLE OF PARDON

In the annals of knowledge long preserved,
A moment wisdom seemed to sway and swerve,
My intellect ascends, a new path to traverse,
A herald of enlightenment, a signal to observe.

Forgiveness, a word of profound acclaim,
Yet do we grasp its essence, its inner flame?
I ask, do we fathom its depths, its name?
Seventy times, forgive, the goddess proclaims.

Have you, dear deity, ever pardoned a soul?
I ponder your judgment, your compassionate role,
For mistakes, spoken words, trust's shattered toll,
To a repentant heart, a pardon is the goal.

This tale unfolds as Nanai did conspire,
We seek warmth as the embers inspire,
The halo, unforgiving, stokes the fire,
In the realms of remorse, we must aspire.

For the deeds, the words, the trust we betray,
To regain love and respect in the light of day,
With unwavering souls, we find our way,
To the realm of forgiveness, where emotions sway.

In every word, each letter's design,
In the spaces between, treasures to define,
Seek the gems, hidden, sublime,
For in the depths, wisdom's light shall shine.

To psychological depths, forever we're led,
By a divine desire that guides us ahead,
In praise and honour, our spirits spread,
As forgiveness prevails, in this epic, it's said.

CHURNING OF THE OCEAN

Behold the ancient myth's grandeur unfolds,
Shimmering costumes in vibrant, shifting molds,
Movements in multi-dimensions are displayed,
I am spellbound, in mystical awe I stay.

Teleportation lifts me to spiritual heights,
Good and evil cast in ritual rites,
Performed each day in routines I live,
Seeking meaning, are my thoughts to give.

Like Mount Mandarah, my focus is fixed,
Tortoise's senses in calm, untroubled mix,
Vasuki guides my divine ascension,
Unlock hidden potential within retention.

Life's churn reveals poison and nectar,
Shadow and ego chart our future vector,
Beyond the mind's control and measure,
Invoke the master to face this dark spectre..

Ego's desire threatens purpose true,

Mephistopheles takes many a form to skew,

Straying from the fountain of the divine brew,

Let your power worldly lures fade through.

CONSTANT SEEKING

My quest for peace is perpetual,
A journey filled with cares habitual,
I strive to leave my past behind,
And leave my troubles far behind.

I search for solace in the night,
But find my mind is still in flight,
I try to find a way to cope,
But fall back into my old scope.

The weight of my regrets and fears,
Is a heavy burden that I bear,
I try to rise above the fray,
But find me falling back to stay.

I long for peace within my soul,
But find my heart is still not whole,
I strive to find a way to heal,
But find myself returning to my old deal.

Yet still I hope, and still I pray,
That one day I'll find my way,
To leave my troubles far behind,
And find the peace I long to find.

A CONSTANT STRUGGLE

As words weigh heavy on my mind
I long to leave this state behind,
Contradictions rise, I can't deny,
I must escape; it's my only guide.

My words are strong, I can't resist,
This rational mode, I can't desist,
Anger builds, I must coexist,
But caution calls, I mustn't persist.

Thoughts unbridled, free and bold,
Without analysis, uncontrolled,
Opponents steady, calm and cold,
I must find balance, I am told.

Oh, divine abode, I seek your grace,
In this constant struggle, I must pace,
To swim to shore, find my place,
And find peace, it's my soul's chase.

This struggle never ends, it's true,
In this sea of change, I must pursue,
A distant shore, a peaceful view,
To rest in peace, my heart anew.

So, I beseech, with humble plea,
A miracle, for the shore to see,
To stretch my arms, to finally be
In your loving bosom, eternally

CREATIVE CELESTIAL CANVAS

Space births new Worlds unseen by humans,
Where stars in unknown constellations rise high.
In cosmic fabric, the universe slowly unfolds,
A canvas boundless where histories mold.

Galaxies are brushstrokes, colors pure 'n bold,
A painter's dream, a story yet untold.
Planets and moons in cosmic dance they spin,
Infinite possibilities as our worlds begin.

In nebulae of wonder, creation flows free,
Gases form stars, mysteries we try to see.
The cosmos' canvas, divine masterwork,
Space the artist, where all elements merge..

And in this grand creation, we take part,
A byproduct of stars' explosive start.
In deep space, where elements combine,
We are stardust, a truth so divine.

From supernova's burst, we came to be,
Recycled star-dust, forged in harmony.
Our DNA, atoms, star remnants,
Links to cosmos, our lives are evident.

Space, the eternal womb, is our true home,
We regenerate, in stardust we grow.
Looking at heavens with awe and delighting,
We see ourselves in vast creation's light.

DANCE OF DECEPTION

In the realm where smiles dance and start,
A heart's affection, a stolen part.
Yet beware, for the venom may impart,
The shocking truth that chills the heart.

Words wrapped in love, a sweet facade,
Transformed to mockery, a bitter clod.
Frozen in the truth, a daunting prod,
The icy grip of love's facade.

Truth in words, in faces worn,
Compassion turning, moments torn.
Cruel twists that leave us mourn,
Terrifying truths, in shadows borne.

Faces wear one, hide another,
A dual dance, a mask to smother.
Praying to honesty, breaking cover,
Away from faces that turn and hover.

Blinding brightness, springtime's grace,
Yet understanding lost, a murky space.
Muddled truths behind each face,
Hidden 'neath a masquerade's embrace.

Looking back with guilt, a heavy load,
Curtains drawn; truths forebode.
Words and expressions deftly sowed,
In time and convenience, a facade bestowed.

In drama's throes, silence learned,
Standing apart, whispers spurned.
Ugliness fades when respect is earned,
Behind backs, the silence yearned.

Continuation, a vow to make,
An act of worth, for love's own sake.
To stand before the Lord, truth to stake,
A sacrifice, a commitment to partake.

A robe of truth, a delicate attire,
Efforts to keep, a sacred fire.
Life's sacrifice on truth's pyre,
An offering to love, lifting higher.

Praise be to the Father, compensation nears,
For dreams petty, and truth's own tears.
Kind one, giver of compassion, quiets fears,
Praise be to you, echo through the years.

DANCE OF SELF-REFLECTION

Selfish it may be, as it journeys free,

Thoughts of its own, in company it seeks,

A lover of itself, it enjoys the dance,

Yet another perspective, in its heart, a chance.

Why does it wander, always in pursuit,

Of its own desires and feelings, resolute?

A mind that yearns, for something unknown,

In its own world, it seeks to be alone.

In isolation and in the ordinary,

It seeks, it seeks, the extraordinary,

A single drop, in the vast sea of time,

In the beauty of connections, it wants to climb.

Surrounded, it stands, by words and more,

Desires, wishes, in its core,

A lively atmosphere, it creates with grace,

But why seek emptiness in this place?

Barnabas Tiburtius § 59

I wonder, my friend,

In each of us, there lies a seed,

That can change, in its own creed,

Without conflict, without strife,

A journey of growth, a change in life.

To understand, to feel and embrace,

The rhythm of life, with style and grace,

A taste, a flavour, a new high,

Revealing the secrets, as we reach for the sky.

The secrets of the night, we unveil,

In the daytime, the stories we tell,

In graduations, we find our way,

Marking the date night, with wisdom, we say,

DANCE OF SOLACE – DECODING EMOTIONAL PARADOXES

A symphony where laughter gently weaves,
A veil, anger's glowing sheaves conceives.
Poised for eruption, embers quietly glow,
Maternal grace, tranquility to bestow.

Shrouded within, a tender warmth persists,
Yet, in this balance, heartbreak persists.
Elusive, undeniable, poignant and rare,
Silently, the journey of solace, I declare.

Words unspoken, a transmission eloquent,
A paradox unfolds, retribution self-sent.
External transgressions, not of my make,
Metamorphose into a self-inflicted ache.

Enjoyment, an art, a call to compose,
A smile carved amidst emotional throes.
Defiance stoic 'against turbulence untamed,
Nuances of serenity, an alliance named.

Amid provocations external, I find,
A mantra of calm, a subtle mind.
Lessons assimilated, a transformation slight,
In the quest for peace, I find my respite.

Feelings, like sentinels, poised with grace,
Tethered to moments that time cannot erase.
Maturity, the crucible, confrontations refine,
Yet, a toll on peace, a lingering sign.

In existence's tapestry, boundaries unfold,
Preordained in chaos, a story foretold.
Upright postures, deliberate gestures weave,
An anchor for minds tumultuous, to believe.

Yet, in this ballet intricate, a divine spectre appears,
Wounds inflicted by life's capricious years.
Fear, intangible spectre, disrupts the serene,
Shattering composure, in mythic tension, seen.

Seizing life's reins becomes imperative,
In the tumultuous sea, a clarion call, declarative.
Why return to peace amidst existence's storm?
A question resonates, a turbulence norm.

The narrative turns, introspective gentle tone,
Life, a penance, willingly undertaken alone.
Accept me wholly, with imperfections in hand,
In this dance of feelings, yearn for grand.

ECHOES OF COMPASSION

After questions fade, challenges cascade,
Restless minds consoled; promises made.
In nods of "Oh well," whose memory weaves,
Words and silence, like shadows that leave.

A refuge in rhythm, last for everyone,
Beauty's rhythm, life's basic spun.
My great love, beyond cause and effect,
Debts of gratitude, in a circle perfect.

Beyond expectations, you've given embrace,
In every movement, your presence we trace.
In humility's gaze, faces unfold,
Many care circles, stories untold.

O great poet, not just words on a page,
But a song sung by humans, an eternal stage.
You, the subject of praise, inner meaning untold,
Compassion and mercy, a love to behold.

ECHOES OF CONNECTION

The thousand stories, questions we confide,
When dear friends meet, emotions amplified,
Voicing untold thoughts, no secrets to hide,
In receptivity's dance, we both reside.

Enthusiasm varies, sometimes denied,
Knocking on locked doors, feelings set aside,
Perception's mirror, truth might be belied,
As thoughts like dust, our vision they've defied.

Our reflections, altered, truth may be denied,
Nature distorted, our relations implied,
In one lifetime's course, wisdom's our guide,
A karmic path, where understanding resides.

With every connection, new meaning to confide,
Incremental refinement, as life does provide,
Reveal the intertwined nature, no need to chide,
In your vast kingdom, cosmic connections tied.

Barnabas Tiburtius § 65

Like a spider weaving, our lives each stride,
A twisted route, design and meaning denied.
Winding down from birth to final death,
To rest in your bosom, cosmic center's breath.

EMBRACING DIVERSE DISCIPLINES

In childhood dreams, on wings of imagination,
With eager heart, I chased each aspiration.
Learn many disciplines, my goal was bright,
To chase the stars, seize day, bask in light.

In science halls, I delved into mysteries deep,
Atoms, cells, galaxies, secrets I keep.
I marvelled at design, from small to grand,
Cosmic wonders vast, I seek to understand.

In ancient lore, I sought wisdom old,
Socrates to Shakespeare, stories made me bold.
Classics, philosophy, art and lofty thought,
Within these treasures abundance I sought.

In art's realm, I painted life in vibrant hues,
A canvas of dreams, hopes, a muse choose.
With brush in hand, I shaped my world anew,
Expressed in colours, every hue true.

The beauty of the human soul I saw,
In strokes of every hue, law and flaw.
In music's tender embrace, melodies I heard,
From Bach to Beatles, symphonies and words.

I danced to rhythms that moved my heart,
In melodies sweet, a soulful art.
The language of the soul in notes I found,
In every beat, in every sound..

Holistic knowledge imbued, infant dreams held tight,
I've grown, flourished, reached new heights in light.
For dreams of youth, now realized, bring grace,
In many fields, I've found my special place.

EMBRACING THE UNSEEN UNIVERSE

In the mind's unrelenting, stifling grasp,
Where shadows play, terrors tightly clasp.
How can a cuckoos metronome call,
Bring lightness to our hearts at all?

Monumental obstacles in our way,
Life, in our path places, day by day.
Yet, a gentle breeze with fragrant air,
Makes burdens in a moment disappear.

Amidst hatred, deceit, and masked faces,
We're trapped in cold, unforgiving places.
Still, a child's innocent smile, pure and bright,
Sets things right and gives us wings in flight.

My love, deceptive are places, you escape,
Where reality bends, takes different shape,
My well-formatted logic may offer its critique,
Unashamed, I make an ungraceful retreat.

Paths in a terrain of multi fold dimensions,
Beyond my comprehension your mansion
But in my soul's desire, with simple grace,
Show existence worth in your embrace.

Compassion reveals a universe unseen,
Where every finite manifestation I glean,
Melts me into formless wave unfathomable,
Merged in your sea of infinite beauty lovable.

ETERNAL LOVE DIVINE

Of love's enduring, timeless grace,
It transcends all time and space,
Binding hearts in sweet embrace,
Eternal as the stars we trace.

Through trials, storms, and darkest night,
Love's flame burns with unwavering light,
Its roots run deep, its reach in flight,
Unyielding, steadfast, pure and bright.

In every whisper, touch, and smile,
Love's essence lingers, all the while,
In every tear, and every trial,
Love's strength prevails, mile after mile.

So let us cherish, honour, and hold,
The eternal nature of love untold,
For in its essence, we find our mould,
A timeless tale, forever bold.

ETERNAL PILGRIMAGE

Bearing our human condition's heavy load,
Through life's intricate, ever-winding road,
In trials and joys, our stories we've sowed,
Our eternal pilgrimage, our souls bestowed.

From cradle's tender touch to life's grand stage,
We enter the world, pure and unmarked page,
With innocence and wonder, we engage,
This human condition, as we come of age.

Through trials and storms, we often find our way,
In darkest nights, we long for break of day,
Our strength is tested as we toil and pray,
Yet through it all, our spirits ever sway.

In times of joy, our hearts do truly swell,
With love and laughter, stories we do tell,
Our shared experiences, a sacred well,
In this human condition where we dwell.

As years go by, we age and we endure,

In time's embrace, we seek what is pure,

Our mortal frames, though fragile and unsure,

Our souls remain, forever strong and sure.

In this eternal pilgrimage we tread,

Our human condition, with wisdom spread,

A journey rich with colours, tears, and thread,

As we bear our human state, our lives are led.

ETERNAL WITNESS – SONG OF THE SENTINEL

In stillness, the old guard, a sentinel so wise,
Twisted branches, sinews reaching the skies.
In the cold night, a phantom sway with grace,
Pointing to stars in the radiant embrace.

Around the relic, barren terrain softly weaves,
Knurled and twisted where the sirocco deceives.
Dew from the sea on antennae so fine,
From thorny branches, a meandering line.

Journeying downward in song so strong,
Droplets pass obstacles, avoiding the wrong.
A thousand roots, aching and parched,
Life's liquid thirst, their hunger to slake.

The Milky Way, a billion stars in cosmic glory,

A timeless task, an ever-fertile story.

Birth from an exploding star, coded in elements,

Nourished in death, with heat so intense.

The old sentinel, witness to cosmic magnitude,

In its silent stance, a timeless gratitude.

EXISTENTIAL LONLINESS

In the vastness of existence,
I am but a tiny speck.
The weight of loneliness presses,
A burden I can barely deflect.

The world around me teems with life,
But I am lost in thought.
The emptiness inside cuts like a knife,
A void that cannot be wrought.

I search for purpose in this world,
For meaning in my strife.
But the answers remain unfurled,
And I am left with this eternal life.

I long for someone to understand,
For a connection that is real.
But it seems I am forever banned,
From finding what I truly feel.

So, I wander through this lonely night,
Hoping to one day find my way.
Until then, I'll endure the fright,
Of this existence that is just okay.

FROM SHADOWS TO LIGHT

As expectations rise with fiery breath,

I teach my mind to ponder, to question why,

When others scale the heights we dream to reach,

I quell impatient thoughts with a knowing sigh.

My heart, caught in its own lamenting sorrow,

Sinks into despair, despite lessons learned,

With courage I draw it out from the dark,

To see the world's pain, and wisdom discerned.

How many desires have I let go,

To reach today's heights, amidst ego's roar,

The struggle to stay above is great,

While pulling back words, once sought to soar.

Unconditional love, easy to speak,

A challenge to weave into thought and deed,

Beyond all measures, let peace be my guide,

O radiant light, in wisdom I heed.

HEART'S COMPASSIONATE QUEST

When the question shifts from many to few,
Who do we know with a heart so true?
In glimpses and shadows, reflections appear,
A stark reality grows, drawing near.

Through fleeting moments and faces blurred,
Stories untold, emotions go unheard.
To understand oneself, the journey begins,
Probing origins deep, where true knowing spins.

Understanding others, a task so rare,
To see through their eyes, a kindred care
A gift for the souls who strive each day,
To forget oneself and look beyond the fray.

Train your mind to hold a heart so wide,
Look upon yourself with kindness inside.
With eyes of love, like a mother's embrace,
See the world anew, with gentle grace.

Boundless light of knowledge guides the way,
Eternal companions on life's grand pathway.
Celebrate clarity as your own,
On this journey of knowing, you've grown.

In love's pure light, together we'll soar,
Understanding deeper, forevermore.

IN PURSUIT OF GENUINE DELIGHT – A SOUL'S ODYSSEY

In the quest for joy, I ponder with a gaze,
The flip side of bliss, a mysterious maze.
Not sadness, I decide, in this heartfelt quest,
Seeking happiness, my spirit is put to the test.

With all that pleases, like others, I try,
Accumulating joy, reaching for the sky.
Yet my mind, averse, turns away and hides,
Behind a forced smile, my true self abides.

Long gone, my happiness echoes others' delight,
A mirror reflection, lost in the night.
Neglecting the question, what truly brings cheer,
I wear a mask, concealing what's dear.

A smile, a facade, my reality deeply hides,
Emotional world like snowflake gently rides.
Before it melts, I guard my pure joy,
In warmth of life, shield from cold's alloy.

Oh great soul, your shaping joy's essence,
Before my birth, a destined presence.
To your lotus feet, I surrender free,
Inner strength you grant me flawlessly.

Praise be to the light, no need for a cure,
Grace untouched by blemish, forever pure.

IN PURSUIT OF IDENTITY

In the realm where beauty's an elusive guise,
A mere semblance, a glimpse that briefly flies,
Love, too, veiled behind a fleeting facade,
Not constant, but like sunlight through the cloud.

Understanding, a semblance, just a trace,
No grand comprehension, it's a fleeting embrace,
Bravery and skill, no fixed, steadfast form,
Unpredictable as a lightning storm's alarm.

All but imitation in this masquerade,
Unique identities in shadows fade,
Life itself mirrors this perplexing game,
Let's live it out, regardless of the fame.

Fear, a creeping vine, spreads its dread,
In the hearts of many, it's widely spread,
In accordance with life's observation,
Filtered, cut, imprinted, in that transformation.

Revealing oneself, a cryptic art,
A reflection of what's within the heart,
Without claiming likeness as one's own,
The true self's identity remains unknown.

Frozen for discernment, a soul does yearn,
To grasp the essence, to truly discern,
Yet, in deep despair, it often seems,
The pinnacle of darkness invades one's dreams.

Amidst the shadows, you emerge, so bright,
A symbol of perfection, day and night,
You grant us insight into the soul's true core,
As a fragment of your mighty self, we implore.

Success and failure, intertwined they be,
As we strive to find our identity,
In this enigma of life's endless quest,
You illuminate the path to our very best.

IN PURSUIT OF TRUTH AND LOVE

I have no heart to lose or stray,
No mirth shall slip or fade away.
With indelible truth, I seek the light,
To shield my eyes, not blind my sight.

In love's fierce battles, brave and true,
Never a by-stander as others do.
I'll acquire my place within the fight,
For humanity's redeeming light.

On this quest to give and receive,
I shed the burden that others grieve.
Holding fast to what matters foremost,
Not seeking gratification at any cost.

For peace of mind, I journey deep and far,
To learn what's right, to know who we are.
Revelation through inner dictates embrace,
An eternal bond, my life's resting space.

Through thorny paths of illusion, we tread,
A lone light guiding us where we're led.
In love's pure song and radiant hue,
I cherish the wonder, deep and true.

IN SEARCH OF NIRVANA

In search of words that speak so deep,
From thoughts profound, my secrets to keep.
In times of noise, where depth is shy,
Silence beckons, yet to express I try.

Life's core, not in chaos do I hanker,
But in simple truths that steady anchor.
Into the dark abyss I tend to fall,
To break the mold to stand tall.

Oh, Love, amidst life's twisted vine,
In shadows deep, my dreams entwine.
My quests, my dreams, I guard with care,
Lest they vanish into the air.

When my being is lost in haze,
I seek my truth in soul's maze,
To touch my essence, pure and kind,
In depths of self, serenity find.

Oh, Divine, may my prayers ascend,
All thoughts and emotions you comprehend,
A soothing balm my aching heart implores,
A healing touch to mend all bleeding pores.

I observe life's never ceasing chase,
As destiny finds its rightful place,
Journey ends, wheel of time comes to rest,
In the matrix of convoluted mind recessed

A liberation I seek from values impressed
A freedom ever unmodulated and expressed
My soul to liberate beyond all ties bound,
For my manifestation, your grace surround.

IN THE EMBRACE OF JOY AND SORROW

A joy and sorrow symphony, composed,
Like a double-edged sword, life enclosed.
Inviting both laughter and tears to flow,
Hand in hand, they touch our heart's core.

No longer opposites, within they stay,
Laughter blooms, while sorrow has its say.
Amidst grief's depth, joy whispers clear,
"Look here, I'm present, always near!"

My mind, a restless soul, it seems,
Moves between extremes, lost in dreams.
Seeking solace in neither, ever adrift,
In motion eternal, by feelings swift.

Oh, beloved, life's canvas can't confine,
For your tender glow has touched the divine.
From this glimpse, a sanctuary I seek,
Where joy and love forever speak.

A shift in view, a subtle turn,
Transforms the mundane to wonders spurned.
Words with twist unveil the hidden,
Language's power never forbidden.

You see my life uniquely bound,
In your presence, solace found.
Divine and radiant, full of grace,
In reverence, I bow, in your embrace.

IN THE HEART OF INFINITE STILLNESS

In the waning light, the sun descends,
Casting shadows long where silence bends.
Amidst the stones, a lone soul stands,
Cloaked in black by time's own hands.

Deep in the heart of the labyrinth's grace,
Concentric spirals trace their place.
The stones, they whisper secrets old,
To the contemplative figure, serene and bold.

The desert stretches, vast and bare,
Yet encircles the soul in gentle care.
A gown flows with the evening breeze,
Binding the dusk in whispered pleas.

Above, the sky a canvas wide,
Brushstrokes of dusk in hues collide.
A spectrum vast, horizon's art,
Reflects the calm within the heart.

In stillness profound, the moment glows,
Echoing thoughts the vastness knows.
The air is thick with what's unsaid,
As light fades, and day is gently led.

Here, amidst nature's silent call,
In the labyrinth's embrace, the answers fall.
The horizon whispers, the soul replies,
In the dusk where the eternal lies.

INFINITE STREAMS OF HOPE

In my mind, a virtual rod unfurls its length,
To measure the space 'twixt two serene shores,
A purpose formed, to calm the torrent's strength,
Within my thoughts, its ceaseless current soars.

As gentle flow swells to mighty flood,
I dip my finger in ground's embrace,
To preserve inner peace, a memory's bud,
Lest it vanish in sun's relentless race.

A damsel bathes each day in this endless stream,
Where beauty dances in serene ambience,
May she savour nature's grace, a tranquil dream,
As one who struggles for a breath, a chance.

Emerging, gasping, from the depths we rise,
Life's meaning is more than just thirst,
Like streams that quench land, in countless ties,
We long for bonds imagined, as we search.

Barnabas Tiburtius § 93

Civilization grows along the fertile streams,
Failing to see the desert's migrating grace.
Mirage becomes our truth, world of dreams,
Erasing fears, we learn to live in this space.

In hope of divine bounty, our hearts unite,
Infinite measures of kindness and of art,
For in each soul, a spark of endless light,
Guides us toward the love that warms the heart.

INVEST ME WITH A MIND TO TRANSCEND

My mind is lost in hopelessness,
Crying out to the one I trusted most,
Why have you abandoned me, my guide?
Leaving me alone in this tumultuous coast.

Nothing can the mother's warmth replace,
When a child feels fear in the unknown,
Similarly, your presence was my solace,
Now I feel like a boat without a loan.

I am not used to this mindset,
If not you, then who else can I trust?
I have no confidence in seeking anyone else,
My faith in you was my only must.

I struggle to find permanence,
Placing my trust in anyone I meet,
But self-doubt always creeps in,
Leaving me in a state of defeat.

Grant me the grace to hold on,
"I will make you fishers of men," You who said,
You are my steadfast anchor,
Invest in me a mind that transcends.

Through constant inner communication,
May I forgive myself and find peace,
With the wisdom you have bestowed upon me,
May my mind's turmoil finally cease.

Oh, guide me to transcend my mind,
And find hope in the darkness that surrounds,
For with you by my side,
I know I can conquer all that astounds.

JEWEL IN THE GARBAGE

Nothing to me, but all to many
Revised priorities, now I see,
Gathered treasures in life's chest,
Judgment gone, my ego at rest.

In your sight, all things are known,
Words and actions, now overthrown,
Garbage heap, a shining jewel,
I hide within, in hope so cruel.

Reluctant, I dispose with care,
In hopes of hiding, it's unfair,
But deluge of waste, I can't escape,
Surrender, I offer, it's no debate.

Adjustments made, compromises too,
All I have, I offer to you,
Fragile life, I accept with grace,
Transformed into shining, divine space.

In total surrender, I bow at your feet,
Imperfections, transformed, so neat,
Imbibing grace, a non-dual bliss,
Shanti, Shanti, Shanti, peace is this.

JOURNEY THROUGH SHADOWS

Amid the shadowed veil of disease's grasp,

We grasp for truth, its origin to clasp,

Inevitable anguish and despair,

Moments of breakdown, hearts laid bare.

I watch in anxious, silent reverie,

Yet, extend your hand, dear child, to me,

With trembling soul, with courage to defy,

A teacher's stern rebuke, though times pass by.

His wisdom lost, like whispers on the breeze,

No justifications found, no sweet release,

An eternal abode of silence, we reside,

In tales untold, self-awareness set aside.

While we unleash our hidden depths in peace,

Who shall discern, within the shifting tides,

As scales of justice sway without remorse,

The game we play, trust in the distant skies.

Barnabas Tiburtius § 99

Even as values change their timeless course,
Oh, deity of ours, we stand and strive,
With resolute resolve, we'll dare and thrive,
In moments such as these, we find our way,
Your presence fades, but we shall not dismay.

In every misstep, we shall still survive,
Depending on ourselves, in truth we thrive,
A medium to be, without haste or chase,
Let your light guide us, in this solemn space.

A bond unbroken, like the stars above,
In the debugger's code, in deepest love,
A brilliant relationship, strong and true,
Our final refuge, I'll stand by you.

JOURNEY TO THE SUBCONSCIOUS

In realms of thought, my greetings sound,
A single note, a truth profound.
Beware the words that falsehood breed,
A monster lurking, most foul indeed.

Beyond mere words, experience lies,
A treasure hidden from prying eyes.
Journeying toward the unexplored,
Lost poems in the mind's hoard.

A dusting of life, a fleeting glance,
Brilliantly glowing in a cosmic dance.
Magic revealed in every chance,
A glorious presence, life's true romance.

Adapt to all, let words subside,
Remove the smallness, let love abide.
Paint an image, rich and wide,
A canvas of emotions, on which we stride.

Root out the poverty in distribution,
Spread love's wealth, a grand resolution.
Fit and more, the gift you bring,
A challenge sent, in feeling's wing.

Billions of pleasures in life entwined,
An eternal dance, forever bind.
Surrounded by smiles, beloved embrace,
In the valley of life, let love find its place.

Soak it in, experience complete,
A symphony of love, oh so sweet.
Kindly look upon me, divine art,
A God protecting the invisible heart.

LAMENTATION OF LIGHT – A DEEPAVALI PRAYER FOR PEACE

In the shimmering glow of Deepavali's light,
Amidst the joy, a solemn plight,
A celebration tainted, a sorrowful sound,
In a world where injustice echoes around.

The festive sky adorned with vibrant hues,
Yet beneath the surface, tears refuse to lose,
For in each burst of fireworks' gleam,
Another life lost, a shattered dream.

In the quiet corners where pain resides,
A heart bears witness to the world's divides,
The innocent souls, victims of strife,
Caught in the crossfire of a turbulent life.

Amidst the colours and the festive cheer,
Lies a truth that many refuse to hear,
In the midst of joy, a cry for peace,
For a world where suffering finds release.

With every cracker that pierces the night,
A plea for mercy takes its flight,
For those whose voices are drowned in war,
May their anguish be felt, near and far.

As delicacies adorn the festive tray,
Let prayers for the hungry not fade away,
In Gaza's shadows, where perennial hunger,
Persists beyond the reach hope still linger.

Let Deepavali be a beacon of light,
Guiding us through the darkest of night,
To stand against injustice, hand in hand,
And bring peace to every troubled land.

With each spark that dances in the air,
May it carry our prayers, our heartfelt share,
For a world where joy knows no divide,
And love, not war, shall forever abide.

LANGUAGE OF SILENCE

Silence speaks volumes, distance forgotten,
One gesture unspoken, yet clear and potent.
Being understood can bring joy or pain,
Misunderstanding becomes norm again.

Even a small whimper from a loving heart,
Can startle and keep us from the start.
Without true communication, we must guess,
Relationships often leave us in distress.

Inner consciousness shines unlike the night,
Revealing truths and removing all doubt.
Relationships come and go, faster than light,
Leaving us to face truth with all our might.

Looking for answers, we search within,
To remove the veil of stifling and imagination,
To see the truth and face it head-on,
And embrace the light of inner realization.

A clear vision to see the true perspective,
Face it bravely, with no objective.
Stare and gaze with all our might,
Praise those who walk this path right.

LEGACY OF LIGHT – A TRIBUTE TO MY SPIRITUAL BROTHER

In the realm of shadows, where memories abide,
A spiritual elder, in the tapestry of time, resides.
Twelve years have passed, yet your essence lingers,
A beacon's glow, in my heart, still flickers.

You, my guide, both teacher and a student true,
Navigating the cosmos, with wisdom imbued.
A dance of roles, a harmonious blend,
In your absence, a void, I can't mend.

Your words, etched in pages, a sacred script,
Each line a compass, a guide well writ,
A legacy of light, penned in a book,
Guiding me, though in your absence I look.

"Be a beacon to the world," your decree,
Echoes through time, a profound decree.
In your absence, I yearn for your embrace,
A spiritual orphan, seeking solace and grace.

Yet, your spirit persists, a radiant flame,
Igniting my soul, though you're not the same.
A mentor, a fan, a paradox so sweet,
In the symphony of life, your melody repeats.

Through the silence, your teachings resonate,
A spiritual inheritance, I contemplate.
I ache for your company, a yearning deep,
In the vastness of loss, your memory I keep.

Oh, elder brother, celestial guide,
In the realms beyond, where spirits abide,
Your legacy lives on, an eternal spark,
Illuminating my journey, through light and dark.

In the tapestry of time, woven with care,
I feel your presence, a spectral heir.
A connection unbroken, a bond that endures,
In my spiritual longing, your essence assures.

LONGING FOR YOU WITH UNTOLD SUFFERING

I'm lost in my thoughts, can't escape this feeling,
My heart's on fire, I'm desperately pleading,
Longing for you, it's consuming my being,
My love for you, it's all-encompassing,

Every moment without you feels like an eternity,
I can't concentrate, you're all I see,
Dreams of us together is all I crave,
My love for you, it's too hard to contain.

Drowning emotions, sowing chaos lay,
This longing for you, it's here to stay.
My heart beats fast, can't catch my breath,
I need you to calm this incessant unrest.

I'll wait for you, no matter how long it takes,
My love for you, it never fades,
I'll endure this pain, till you're by my side,
My heart feels like exploding, I can't hide.

MENDING MINDS – THE POWER OF POSITIVE AFFIRMATIONS

In mind's chambers, where shadows dwell,
Lies power to transform, make thoughts swell.
Positive affirmations, a healing embrace,
Mend wounded souls, find peaceful space.

With whispers gentle, kind words we send,
Mending fragments, soothing troubled blend.
"I am strong, I am brave," they flow,
Through storms turbulent, let healing grow.

At dawn's quiet, as the world awakes,
Sunbeams of affirmation our spirit takes.
"I am worthy, I am loved," we breathe,
Mending hearts and fears we believe.

In despair's depths, when hopes fade,
"I am resilient, I am whole," I've stayed.
With positivity's, we mend every seam,
Healing our minds, dispelling haunting dreams.

In turmoil of thought, doubts rise in vain,
"I am confident, I am free," they shine.
Mending fractured spirits, every fragile piece,
Embracing healing, finding deep inner peace.

Speak kindly to ourselves, honest and true,
Healing with words, affirmations imbue.
"I am grateful, I am kind," let these guide,
Riding through life with hearts open wide.

NATURE'S RESILIENT SYMPHONY

Beneath the dim Sunlight's feeble rise we stand,
A forest of pines, bare bones of the land,
Few leaves linger on these skeletal trees,
Deprived of chlorophyll, in chilling breeze.

Yellowish light dances with the wind's cruel grace,
Like darts of needles, nature's chilling embrace,
Winter's breath, a merciless, cold thief,
Depriving life of energy, causing grief.

Yet nature waits, patient in its stand,
For the harsh winter to release its hand,
The cosmic dance of Earth's wobbling song,
Promises another spring before long.

The Sun, in former glory, shall blaze anew,
Bringing warmth and life, to all that grew,
Revitalizing every tree, with gentle touch,
Awakening the creatures, who slumbered as such.

In sheltered rest, they famished lie,
Yearning for the grasslands to come alive,
For the silent birds to sing in harmony,
A joyful chorus, to greet the spring's decree.

OLD SENTINEL IN THE DESERT

There stood a silent, rooted, unmoving sentinel.

Barren twigs varied shapes, stretching skyward.

In the cold night, a phantom swaying high.

Pointing to stars that sparkle in the sky.

Morphing reality where shapes change

As move around a vision to behold.

Knurled, twisted by age stripped and bare.

Soft outer hiding the tough core inside.

Dew drops from sea blown by dry wind.

Find solace resting on tiny sharp antennae.

From lofty thorny branches, journey begins.

Viscous flow moves in measured, slow steps.

Droplets fuse downward from nearby branches.

Overcoming each undulation and crevice.

Roots wait patiently beneath the dry ground.

Lips parched for life-giving liquid's embrace.

Drops quickly extract from dry sandy soil.

Before hunger of scorched land consumes all.

Milky Way with stars arches in glory.

Her cosmic vault, timeless mother's fertile task.

Ancient tree born in shifting elements.

Routed from a star's explosive creation.

Needing sustenance in relentless, scorching heat.

The sentinel stands silent, never to retreat.

PIERCED AND WOUNDED – A BROKEN SOUL'S CRY

In a father's heart, can silence find a place,
As his child pleads, a supplication with grace.
A mother's heart, can it a cry, mournful, endure,
When her daughter weeps, for a demand pure.

In humble plea, not entitled but to demand,
O my Lord, life's grandeur, before your door, I stand.
A beggar, your compassion, seeking alms divine,
With tears that resonate, like a sacred shrine.

What are my boundaries, how far can I extend?
Who holds the highest place for me to transcend?
I found an answer to this question swiftly.
My beloved's thoughts are limitless and lively.

Whatever, whenever, wherever you decree,
In restless prayer, I seek nectar as a honeybee.
Head bowed, mind swaying, on your shoulder lean,
Nagging you, asking, "How much longer? When?"

Be patient with my plea, O benevolent guide,
As a child returning, joyous surprise inside.
Home from study, tired and worn,
In life's changing scenes, your actions are born.

Overwhelm me with joy, surprises unfold,
In the tapestry of life, your wonders untold.
Give me shadows of hope, a reason to exist,
O great ocean of love, in your embrace, I enlist.

Mother's heart, generous beyond measure,
Granting all asked for, a boundless treasure.
O wonder, praise, praise, in your glory I sing,
To the symphony of love, let my gratitude ring.

POWER OF LOVE

In the depth of my being, I feel it's might,
A force that inspires and makes all things right.
An unyielding power born of love's embrace,
That sets forth a change and transforms our fate.

It gives us the strength to push through the pain,
To endure, to persevere, to begin once again.
A beacon of hope that guides us through the night,
A light that illuminates our hearts with its might.

Love gives us a reason to keep moving on,
An inspiration to fight until the battle is won.
It binds us together, connecting heart to heart,
Giving us the courage to make a brand-new start.

With love in our hearts, we can conquer all fears,
Vanquish all doubts and wipe away all tears.
It shows us the path to our true destiny,
And lifts us up from the depths of our misery.

So let us embrace the power of love,

And soar to the heavens, on wings like a dove.

For within its embrace, we will find our way,

To a life filled with purpose and joy each day.

QUEST FOR ENLIGHTENMENT

An epic tale unfolds before me,
Of love and passion, raw and true.
A quest for enlightenment, a journey,
Through the tangled forest, to find the way through.
With each step, my heart and mind are free.

A search for self, to shed the weight,
Of doubts and fears, that bind and hold.
To see the world with new eyes,
And break the chains, that make me old.
With each breath, my spirit takes flight.

The Bodhi tree, a symbol of peace,
A beacon of hope, in the dark of night.
Under its branches, I find my release,
And in its shade, my soul takes flight.
With each thought, my mind is at ease.

The reins of life, I hold in my hand,
And guide my path, with steady tread.
Through the trials and the tribulations,
I find the strength, to rise ahead.
With each step, my heart takes command.

And in my weakness, I find my strength,
In the words that I compose and speak.
With each line, I find new meaning,
And in the end, my soul is free.
With each breath, my heart takes wing.

REFLECTING YOUR ABUNDANCE

A heart that's pure and true,
With love for all, it shines so bright,
A light that guides through every plight,
For one whose happiness is everyone's delight.

He feels the pain of those in grief,
And sheds a tear for their relief,
Through such a person, the universe is blessed,
For they are truly the best.

What are my boundaries, how far can I extend,
Who holds the highest place for me to transcend?
I found an immediate answer to this query,
My beloved, whose thoughts are limitless and lively.

Knowing that infinitude truly belongs to me.
Longing intense beat within the divine heart.
All obstacles are negated and erased.
Knowing the secret, you wait for me.

Barnabas Tiburtius § 123

With a smile that blooms majestically.
Joyful and heavenly, all feels so divine.
Wisdom begins in you, the prime mover.
In your love, I find my true lover.

With feathers on my wings, I'll fly,
To your realm of unmitigated passion, oh my!
Not realizing, it is in your vehicle, I reside,
Forever in your love, my soul will abide

RIVERS OF VERSE – NAVIGATING THE POET'S SOUL

In realms obscure, what else to write,
Stunned by that, horrified, the poet's plight.
My verses flow, an endless stream,
A ceaseless current, an elusive dream.

In the mountain of creation, a breath so deep,
Deciding what to carve, what secrets to keep.
Slow down, oh soul, in this poetic quest,
A river of life, flowing at its own behest.

Deficiencies and biases, a selfish scrawl,
Narrowed circles, friendships take a fall.
Straightening the neck of strained relations,
A dance of balance, life's fluctuations.

Smiles once great, now a distant trace,
Forgiveness given, a transformative grace.
Magic whispers, altering the mind's course,
Lightening burdens with a mysterious force.

Oh beloved, the murky flood's embrace,
All senses struggle for calming solace,
Darkness within, a relentless fight,
Torn pages of the mind, seeking the light.

A small smile, a healing potent potion,
Moments as medicine, a soothing lotion,
Gently applied over the senses five,
A relieving balm, pain to abate strive.

Somewhere a smile will brilliantly shine,
Opportunities sought, love to define.
Dust rises within, a turbulent tide,
Blown away with force, shadows subside.

Trying and losing, the old darkness bows,
Conquering the mind, as determination allows.
In lean periods, with no delay,
Surrendering to the journey, come what may.

An effulgence. radiant, a song so grand,
Praise echoes, an anthem across the land.
In the esoteric dance, life's poetic maze,
A hymn to existence, through myriad days.

SEEDS OF LOVE IN A GARDEN OF HATRED

In hearts ensnared by hatred's bitter bane,

I seek a plot for love's sweet seed to gain.

Despair, a silent spectre, haunts my gaze,

As innocence succumbs to toxic haze.

A crowd, suspicious eyes cast all around,

In ignorance, discerns not love profound.

Devotion tangled with the thorns of doubt,

A garden fraught with queries, left without.

Shocked, I witness cruelty's vile quakes,

As hearts, once bound by love, begin to break.

Yet, in this maelstrom, love, my dear,

Longs to shun the poison that draws near.

A forest blooms with fury uncontrolled,

Discarding virtues, friendship, truth, and gold.

When love, a beggar, pleads for what's due.

Smiles measured, masking layers through.

In despair, as humanity's end draws near.

Silent inaction chains us, breeds our fear.

Yet amidst gloom, you offer a bloom.

A delicate flower in looming doom.

Softness bestowed when weapons demand.

A paradox of care within love's hand.

To the great love, that steadfast force,

Whether present or a phantom's course,

I pray, plant hope's seed in soil untamed,

Awaiting smiles in hearts, once confused,
reclaimed.

SEEKING SERENITY – A JOURNEY OF SELF-DISCOVERY

In restless moments, we seek in earnest desire.

We crave for objects no forethought or reason.

Not satisfied, we search again for more.

Not content, we wallow in endless dissatisfaction.

A roving vagabond on unceasing wave.

Seldom tarrying to appreciate true experience.

Unaware objects held hidden higher values.

Discarded, objects had meanings left unseen.

Illuminate my mind, break limited boundaries.

In divine light, taste sweetness's pure essence.

Embedded in all creation's sacred pattern.

I beg for grace to wake me from sleep.

That dulls my mind, shrouded in ignorance.

Grant visitation to merge my limited self.

So I can find peace in this life.

In endless quest for fleeting satisfaction's call.
We lose treasures within our daily reach.
Chasing distant dreams and distant shores.
Missing the beauty of present love's glow.

Teach me to find contentment each hour.
Seek wisdom in pure and simple form.
In your light, I find my power.
To cherish the world and brave life's storm.

Let me not be a vagabond lost in endless pursuit,
But rather, let me be a wanderer of the heart,
Discovering the joy in each moment, resolute,
And from your grace, may I never depart.

SEEKING WINGS IN THE GRIP OF TIME

Though we know all ends in time,
Eternity we still pursue,
An endless race we run and run,
But what the goal, we cannot see.

In joy we drown, yet still we know
That joy will end, and all is vain,
In sorrow we are lost and blind,
And hope of rising we disdain.

Is joy the symbol of our lives,
That fade away like morning mist.
Is sorrow the great mystery,
That spreads to infinity?

My love, you show me all the world,
The universe, are but a pair,
Of joy and sorrow, hand in hand,
That bind our lives and make us care.

We try to grasp the unattainable,
And spoil the air with our desires,
We stain the breath of life with dust,
And twist our lives to fit our fires.

But you, my love, you show me true,
That in the midst of joy and pain,
The soul can soar to greater heights,
And leave behind the bonds of fate.

You guide me on my journey,
To heights beyond my wildest dreams,
To new horizons, new beginnings,
To greater things, my soul, my themes.

O great one, O saintly one, O wonder,
I praise you, praise you, evermore,
For showing me the way to fly,
Beyond the bounds of time and space.

Barnabas Tiburtius § 133

SILENCE AS A GIFT

Silence speaks, though words are scarce,
A fossil stands, emotions still in place,
A seed is sown, with hope to bear,
But unexpected growth brings a sudden grace.

A search begins, to right the course,
But anchors slip, thoughts lose control,
Desperation leads to impulsive force,
Deviating further from the intended goal.

But in this stillness, a profound peace,
A silent language that divinity will release,
The noise and chaos fade away,
Like moonlight on calm waters, serene display.

Your gift of life, with love in sight,
Fills me with humanity, so pure and bright,
The gift of silence, like a balm so sweet,
Leads me to your presence, complete.

So, heed not ego's clamour and lead,

To this realm of silence, where I'll be freed,

From the turmoil and noise of life's strife,

With your love and grace, a new way of life.

SOUL'S LUMINANCE

In search of what ignites my spirit's flame,
Patti Smith's wisdom, a guiding star to claim,
Through William Blake, her inspirations rise,
To elevate my soul, expand my skies.

Who are the beings, ideas that lend me wings,
To soar beyond the mundane, where silence sings?
They're muses, dreams, in pages, art, and thought,
Magnifying my spirit, they are sought.

In books, profound, the whispers of the wise,
I find the echoes of immortal skies,
I cherish their words, their essence, and their grace,
With every line, my soul finds its own place.

These influences, they are my cherished boon,
A vaccine for my spirit, a radiant tune,

Not just a cure for life's unholy trials,
But shields that guard my spirit's sacred miles.

In each encounter, my vitality is renewed,
In beauty and wisdom, I'm deeply imbued,
With those who magnify my spirit's might,
I'm wrapped in radiance; my soul takes flight.

So, seek the flames that keep your soul ablaze,
In pages, art, in wisdom's endless maze,
They're the guardians of your inner light,
Magnify your spirit, keep your radiance bright.

STANDING IN AWE

The mountains stand tall and grand,
Awe-inspiring and strong,
Their peaks reach for the sky,
Where eagles sing their song.

The birds that call these peaks home,
Soar on wings of grace,
Their freedom is a sight to see,
In this wild and wondrous place.

I stand below these giants,
My mind and body small,
But my spirit soars with the birds,
As I gaze upon them all.

My desire is to be like a mountain,
Reaching for the sky,
When unable your image I frame,
Seeking union, a reality nigh.

The creator has bestowed.
Such beauty on this land,
The mountains and the birds,
Are a wonder to behold and stand.

I am grateful for this creation,
And the gifts it brings,
May I always stand in awe,
Of the mountains and their wings.

STARDUST TO SAPIENS

Stardust to Sapiens, a journey profound,
From cosmic beginnings to life on the ground.
Infinite galaxies, stars burning bright,
A cosmic ballet in the vastness of night.

From dust and gas, the universe's dream,
Building blocks of life, or so it would seem.
Nebulae birthed us in their fiery grace,
We are stardust collated in infinite space.

Eons passed by, as we started to grow,
Life's tender shoots in the primordial glow.
From simple cells, in oceans they swam,
Life's evolution, a grand cosmic plan.

Through the ages, we evolved and changed,
Surviving and thriving in nature's wide range.
With each tiny step, our minds grew,
From bacteria to ones who much knew.

Stardust to Sapiens, a story unfolds,
Of minds that ponder, of stories untold.
From hunter and gatherer to cities of steel,
Our intellect's journey, a remarkable ordeal.

Language and culture, knowledge and art,
We reached for the stars; we conquered the chart.
Our quest for understanding, an infinite quest,
From stardust to sapiens, we are truly blessed.

But let's not forget, reaching for sky,
We're made of stardust, to stardust we'll fly.
In cosmic tapestry, we play a part,
From universe birth, till creation depart.

Stardust to Sapience, a journey profound,
In the cosmos, life on this blue dot found
Our place in the universe, a grand mystery
A grand design we' create our history.

SUBMERGED IN NATURE

It is a great feel to be in this verdant terrain,

Trees stand like soldiers with their lance,

The creepers climb for a better view,

This passing soul filled with serenity,

Silence parading the green tapestry,

Flowers smiling in radiant display,

Multiple, variegated hues dancing in the wind,

Gentle rocking, a lullaby for the tired soul,

Birds perched in low branches tweet,

A hidden code communicating Joy,

A few hunger-driven, pecking in the grass,

To pull out a worm or a resting insect,

Dragon Flies their translucent wings display,

Spectacular in the low flashing sunlight,

I walk the Rose Garden an exhilarating mix,

Of colours and smell that hangs low,

To my perceiving senses. a well spread feast,

A thousand Bees humming, a waning buzz,

As they near the nectar laden abode,

A symphony when intently listened.
This assembly in its communication,
My heart beats in synchronous rhythm.
Connections of love pour forth in abundance,
My heart overflows in supreme joy unmitigated.

TENDER HEARTS – STRONG MINDS

In a world where storms may brew,

Let smiles and hints calm you through.

Joy's promise, hope's steadfast light,

Guiding through life's darkest night.

A gaze so kind, a vow unsaid,

Gifts from hearts, compassionate thread.

Forgiveness pleads from depths unknown,

Finding solace in warmth shown.

Oh, my love so dear and true,

My words for you, pure and new.

Evil's shadow blocks the way,

But light will come, like the day.

Open wide your heart's embrace,
Let light in, and judgement replace.
Eager for each morning's rise,
Treasures found in gladdened eyes.

Take my hand, and with me, stand,
In the sanctuary of our land.
Solace, refuge, thoughts that bind,
In this marvel, peace we find.

THE ALCHEMY OF FORGIVENESS

In any bond of depth and significance,
Forgive, forgive, forgive, the heart's defence.
The richest relationships, life's elegant dance,
Are lifeboats, submarines, with soul's recompense.

They descend to the depths, disquieting places,
Unfathomed trenches where our innermost races.
Our shames, vulnerabilities, hidden faces,
Forgiveness is the key to these secret spaces.

The alchemy of shame into honour's embrace,
A privilege to see each other's true face.
Witnessing darkness with love's gentle grace,
Forgiveness, the light in this sacred space.

Buoyancy's engine, forgiveness' sweet chore,
Submarine rising, towards the light once more.
From darkness to lifeboat, love's open door,
Forgive and forgive, our spirits restore.

THE ART OF STILLNESS

In the rush of life's ceaseless flow,
Build pockets of stillness, let them grow.
Meditate in the quiet of your mind,
In solitude and peace, your spirit find.

Go for walks, in nature's embrace,
Let the world's chaos gently erase.
Ride your bike, with no destination in sight,
Embrace the freedom, let your soul take flight.

Daydreaming holds a creative key,
Unleashing thoughts that are wild and free.
From boredom, sparks of brilliance ignite,
In the canvas of the mind, ideas take flight.

Don't force the muse, let it come to you,
In the depths of your being, it'll imbue.
Unconscious thoughts in combinations anew,
Give birth to creativity, in all that you pursue.

Barnabas Tiburtius § 147

Sleep, oh sleep, the creator's best friend,
Where dreams and visions endlessly blend.
Aphrodisiac for the mind, so profound,
In its rest, inspiration can be found.

It guides your day, sets your rhythm's pace,
Mends your spirit, grants a peaceful space.
From negativity, it offers a retreat,
Ensuring your emotions and thoughts are sweet.

Be disciplined in your rest, make it a creed,
As vital as the air that you breathe.
For wearing tiredness as a badge is in vain,
Your health and sanity, above all, sustain.

Your priorities must be clear and bright,
For from them, your world takes flight.
Embrace the art of stillness, let it be,
The source of your creativity, wild and free.

THE BATTLE AGAINST CYNICISM

In the chambers of our hearts, we find a beast,
A cynic, lurking, ready to unleash its feast,
But we won't let it hold us in its snare,
For we'll fight cynicism, and life's burdens bear.

In ourselves, we'll thwart its creeping might,
With noble doubt and reason shining bright,
Not stagnant, but growing, we'll find our way,
To a place where cynicism cannot sway.

With those we love, we lead by example true,
Kindness and empathy in all that we pursue.
Cynicism hides as something grand,
Unmasked through wisdom we understand.

Unlike the dark, corrosive force it tends to be,
We'll nurture spirits, set our hearts and minds free,
Our faith in humankind, a beacon in the night,
A counterforce to cynicism's blight.

Barnabas Tiburtius § 149

In this world that often seems to drift astray,
We'll stand with courage, in a largehearted way,
With sincerity, we'll let our spirits soar,
And cynicism's grip, we shall ignore.

So, let us rise, with resilience and defiance,
Fight cynicism with unwavering reliance,
For in hope and growth, we'll surely find,
The antidote to cynicism, for all of humankind.

THE BIRTH OF A VERSE

The birth of a verse
Is a magical sight,
Far more than the dawn
Of the lengthy night.

Through lifetimes it lingers,
In quiet persist,
Choosing its moment,
When it cannot resist.

A verse's not born
From the minds we hold dear,
But from corners of cosmos,
Far, bright, and clear.

It selects us as vessels,
Its path to the world,
With mysteries ancient,
In verses unfurled.

The depth of our lives
Is the key to this art,
For it moulds and it shapes,
Each beat of our heart.

When we delve ever deeper,
In life's grand design,
The verse emerges,
In form refined.

Like dreams of a child,
Crimson and bright,
Nourished by saffron,
In milk's warm light.

We shape our perspectives,
Far from the norm,
In dreams of great verses,
We're profoundly transformed.

Oh, grand beloved,
The force so divine,
Reveals simple truths,
In poetic line.

It bids us refine
Our lives with its grace,
To harmonize contradictions,
In soft embrace.

Oh, vast wonder,
That chose me to sing,
Through cosmos's expanse,
Its truths to bring.

THE BLOSSOMING OF TIME

In world of haste and instant gain,
Debbie's wisdom, a timeless refrain:
"Expect worthwhile things do take time,"
For patience and perseverance in our climb.

Myth of overnight success, a fleeting dream,
True success is not what it may seem.
Triumph's definition needs thoughtful rewrite,
For in the journey, our strength takes flight.

The flower's beauty, from bud to bloom,
Doesn't happen in a single afternoon.
Culture loves the flashy, outward display,
Ignoring tedium, true growth finds its way.

The magic of life unfolds in steady steps,
In choices we make, in words left unsaid.
Our character, destiny we shape each day,
Products of patience paved in a unique way.

Cherish the blossoming, a steady grind,
True treasures of the soul we find.
In wisdom of patience, we'll finally see,
The worth of endurance, in you and me.

THE CUSTODIAN OF INTEGRITY

In the wisdom of Angelou, we confide,
When they unveil their souls, we must not deride,
Yet when they attempt to define who we are,
We mustn't be swayed by opinions bizarre.

The custodian of our integrity, we stand,
Amidst the judgments, we'll still command,
For those who misconceive what we hold dear,
Their assumptions reveal, it's crystal clear.

Presence, a masterful, intricate art,
Not mere productivity, right from the start,
In a culture that worships wealth and gain,
In the pursuit of joy, we must not wane.

For the cult of productivity, it has its place,
But devotion to it, we must gracefully embrace,
Without losing the wonder that life can unfold,
As Annie Dillard's words, so beautifully told.

In the tapestry of days, we weave our lives,

Amidst productivity, our spirit thrives,

In the balance of both, we find our grace,

As the custodian of integrity, we embrace.

THE DANCE OF MIND'S EVOLUTION

In world where opinions thrive and sway,
Culture's weight on what we think, we say.
Allow yourself the luxury to change,
Embrace the mind stray, fleeting, strange.

Cultivate that capacity, negative and wise,
To question and to learn, to scrutinize,
For it's not in stubbornness that we excel,
But in the realms where open minds can dwell.

We often wear opinions, like a cloak,
Yet, they're borrowed, hardly bespoke.
Invest time, let convictions bloom,
In your mind, where wisdom finds room.

Let go of anchors, cling not to the past,
For truths can change, beliefs are not the last,
Say, "I don't know," embrace the mystery,
And you will find the world's rich tapestry.

It's more rewarding, understanding's grace,
To shift and grow, in mind's embracing space,
Embrace the change in thought, ideology's shelf,
And most of all, evolve within yourself.

THE GIFT OF GENEROSITY

In life's grand tapestry, we find our place,
To shine our light, to share our warm embrace,
Be generous with time, let kindness unfurl,
For it's the key to a more loving world.

In every moment, let your spirit soar,
With open heart, let compassion outpour,
With giving credit, honour others' worth,
We foster bonds that span the bounds of Earth.

Embrace your words as tools for love and praise,
A song of grace, through life's meandering maze,
It's easier to criticize and negate,
But celebration, let's cultivate.

Each critique, a story, there's a soul behind,
A fragile heart, a thoughtful, creative mind,
To understand, to be understood, our aim,
Life's greatest gifts, we all can claim.

Each interaction, a chance to bestow,
The gifts of empathy, let kindness flow,
For human threads weave life's tapestry,
In generous exchange, we find unity.

THE IDEALIST'S CALL

In a world that craves the cat GIF's delight,
Don't be afraid, embrace the guiding light,
Idealist's heart, a beacon burning bright,
Creators of culture, let us take flight.

Are we to bow to demands already known,
To cater, pander, in this world we're thrown,
Or stand with White, the seeds of truth be sown,
To lift people up, a path less trod upon.

With increasing urgency, we must heed,
Each cog in society, plant the righteous seed,
Supply the substantive, fulfil the need,
To foster a culture where ideals may feed.

The road to success, they say, is paved with care,
But true progress comes from those who dare,
To rise above the trivial, the superficial snare,
To nurture the ideal, a future bright and fair.

For in this dance of culture, dynamic and bold,

We have the power, the stories to be told,

To be creators, not just consumers in the fold,

As idealists, let our vision take a hold.

So don't be afraid, let your ideals be bold,

In world of needs, latent suffering untold,

Lift people up, let your ideals swell,

In the dream called culture, be an idealist pearl.

THE TORTUOUS PATH

Through the thicket of complexity,
I struggle to find my way,
The tortuous path before me,
Full of knots that led astray.

I try to slip away unscathed,
But the knots won't let me be,
Conveniently I forget,
That they're a part of me.

I stand and observe in wonder,
What can I do to be free?
I dare to criticize and ponder,
The answer lies within me.

With patience, I unravel,
The elements that hold me tight,
I discard the easy path,
And fight with all my might.

An escape I hope to find,
From this tortuous path I tread,
But I know deep down inside,
It's a journey I must not dread.

The fundamental approach I take,
Guides me through life's strife,
But its futility I cannot fake,
It's an anchor in the sea of life.

So, I extend my mighty arm,
And impart some understanding,
The knots that cause us harm,
Are a part of our own doing.

To trace the path to our abode,
We must face the knots with grace,
For they're the tortuous road,
That leads us to our rightful place.

THE TRUE PURSUIT

Do nothing for prestige's fleeting gleam,
Nor status, money, nor fleeting dream.
For Paul Graham's wisdom speaks with truth,
Prestige can warp the core of youth.

Extrinsic drives, they may feel fine,
But deeper purpose, not on that line.
Life's true rewards are found within,
Where deeper meaning does begin.

Don't chase the things that fade away,
In morning's light or night's last ray.
Instead, seek purpose, passion, and delight,
In those, you'll find the lasting light.

The thrill of waking, the night's embrace,
Are found in purpose's gentle grace.
Detract from hollow, shallow aims,
Embrace the depth, where true life flames.

THREADS OF RESOLVE AND REVELATION

In all my capacity I gather the remnants,
Echoes of time, whispers of the past,
A mosaic of moments, a kaleidoscope,
A journey through memories, fleeting and vast.

With an intention that all my energy
Shall converge like rivers to the sea,
A singular purpose, a luminous beam,
Guided by purpose, a soul's decree.

Should with laser sharp focus target
Every aspiration, every noble goal,
Cutting through the fog of doubt,
A beacon in the night, a shining soul.

With no cursed distraction be redeemed,
A pledge to silence the sirens' call,
To stay the course, unwavering,
Resisting the tempest, standing tall.

The constant threat from past psychic imprints,
Ghosts that linger, shadows in the mind,
Yet, I rise with courage, steadfast,
A seeker of truth, no longer blind.

Unlocking aberrations, a deliverance sought,
From the chains that bind, the echoes of pain,
A metamorphosis, a rebirth,
Emerging from darkness, breaking the chain.

Till my resolve formulated as intent,
Solid as the mountains that touch the sky,
A fortress of will, unyielding,
In the face of challenges, I will not shy.

A possibility assumed an easy mission,
Yet, the path unfolds with twists and turns,
A labyrinth of choices, a cosmic dance,
In each step, a lesson, each lesson, wisdom earns.

Now I stand in awe, this insurmountable task,
A mountain to climb, a sky to explore,
Yet, with each step, with each breath,
I discover strength I never knew before.

You who is the beginning and the end,
The cosmic weaver, the orchestrator of fate,
In your cosmic dance, a cosmic ballet,
A timeless story, an eternal mate.

You birthed me from a remote vastness,
A stardust child in the cosmic sea,
With the cosmic wind as a lullaby,
A manifestation of divine mystery.

In this manifestation, abode of enigmatic game,
A playground of stars, a dance of light,
I navigate the maze, the cosmic chessboard,
In pursuit of truth, in the quest for insight.

Seek a revelation of this ageless mystery,
The riddle of existence, the puzzle of time,
In the cosmic library, pages turn,
A seeker of truth, in this cosmic paradigm.

A block to revealing light, unable to pierce,
The veil of illusion, the shadows' play,
Yet, with unwavering faith, I persevere,
To unveil the truth, to find the light of day.

Unknown darkness a karmic projection,
A cycle to break, a pattern to mend,
With the sword of awareness, the shield of intent,
I march forward, on destiny's road to transcend.

I stand in deep yearning for illuminating revelation,
A pilgrim in the temple of cosmic grace,
Yearning for the truth, the divine invitation,
To embrace the light, to see the unveiled face.

THREADS OF VANITY – LOSS OF IDENTITY

In the realm of taste, flavours dance 'n play,
Once joyous sensations now seem far away.
The heart, once stirred by culinary delight,
Now finds itself in a silent, empty night

Clothes, once chosen for others' eyes to see,
Now hang forgotten, devoid of vanity.
No longer worn to impress or allure,
They gather dust, their purpose unsure.

Money and wealth, once prized and sought,
Now cling to me, their grip a tangled knot.
Yet I feel no urge to grasp and hold tight,
For they offer no solace in the quiet of night.

Fame, with its fleeting and hollow pride,
No longer tempts me to ride its fickle tide.
My head remains unbowed, my spirit free,
For true fulfilment lies beyond what eyes can see.

For in this vast expanse we call life's domain,
One thing alone can ease the heart's pain.
It is the love that knows no bounds or measure,
The balm that brings true joy and treasure.

My beloved, in your embrace I find,
The culmination of all I've sought to find.
In your touch, a profound realization,
That love alone is life's true foundation.

Your smile, a beacon of hope and grace,
Lights up my world, brings warmth to my face.
In your love, I find supreme bliss,
And in your presence, all else I dismiss.

So let us sow the seeds of love far and wide,
In every heart where emptiness resides.
For in love's embrace, we find our true worth,
And await the harvest of love's boundless mirth.

TO BE A WORTHY TEACHER

Pretentious practices and ritualistic postures,
Dramas and compromises, the masks we wear,
An appendage perennial to ourselves,
Glued through injustice and compromise,
Cast in the mould of truth and a transgress,
Has become a rudderless way of life.

The resultant mindset hijacks our attitude,
From a mentor to a manipulator of young lives,
Like a life held tight to our own identity,
Our tutelage, is corrupt to the slaving intent,
They are distanced from an empowering reality,
Without the courage to face the complex world.

Living in this falsehood in the ruptured craft,
Instead of life saving raft or a floating lifebuoy,
A mill stone tied to sink in false comfort,
To a descent of eternal, fathomless doom,
We consign our children in a false mindset,
Never to taste the sweet nectar of truth.

Can we be rid of this sin of a direction false,

Not deserving the holy title of teacher or guru,

I beseech you, Oh holy architect of wisdom,

For an ablution of forgiveness and compassion,

To renew my knowledge, a baptized state, pure,

Plant the seed of hope to blossom, a worthy
mentor.

TREASURES BEYOND PLEASURES

In the tapestry of life's grand design,
Treasures hidden, gems divine,
To realize their worth, we must perceive,
Beyond mere trade, where values cleave.

The heart of value transcends the gold,
It's in the stories silently told,
Layers of creation, artist's intent,
Each element, a message sent.

Priceless essence, hidden desire,
A spark, a flame, a burning fire,
Unveiling truth, a fervent quest,
In each detail, we find what's best.

Like a sandcastle on the shore,
Fleeting moments, here no more,
Life's swift dance before our eyes,
As the passing wave, it flies.

Amidst this chaos, I stand still,
Searching for a purpose, an inner thrill,
Like a monkey, I leap and swing,
Yet miss the taste of a single thing.

A multitude of fruits I've tried,
But in the chase, the core denied,
Grant me wisdom, deep and true,
To savour life's sweet nectar too.

In moments fleeting, I'll find grace,
And in your light, I'll see your face,
Enlightenment, a path to choose,
To be grateful, and my soul to lose.

In your divine embrace, I'll thrive,
In fullness and gratitude, I'll dive,
For the treasures of life, I'll see,
Blessed by your grace, eternally free

THE UNVEILING OF FORGIVENESS

In realms of knowledge, steadfast and secure,
There comes a moment, a mystery obscure,
When in doubt, question that you've known,
A signal of growth in the seeds of the unknown.

Forgiveness, a word, as high as the sky,
Do you fathom its depths? Can you tell me why?
Forgive me, they say, seventy times and more,
Have you pardoned so as to open heart's door?

Mistakes made, words said, hearts do fray,
Trust shatters, love's warmth fades away,
Yet to the soul that begs for mercy's sweet kiss,
Remember, compassion is not one to dismiss.

Is it me in my wisdom so grand,
We warm our souls in forgiveness's hand,
The halo of grace, forever it spins,
Forgiveness, the balm that heals all our sins.

In actions, in words, in the depths of the heart,
Forgiveness is art, a masterful part,
Seek in the spaces between letters and lines,
Treasures of pardon, through heart's love shines.

To reach the same state, without hesitation,
Forgiveness brings peace, a divine revelation,
In every word's echo, in letters that bind,
A psychological depth, the soul's path to find.

In the pursuit of treasures, don't hide or pretend,
Let forgiveness guide you, as a steadfast friend,
For in knowledge's embrace, both old and anew,
The desire divine, forever in you.

UNVEILING THE MELODY OF LIFE

This life's own song, my chosen art,

I sing it true, with all my heart.

No faltering beat, no rhythm wrong,

My voice's sweetness lingers long.

Like spring's pure essence, deep and bright,

My song brings cool in shades of night.

Who hears, who shuns, who holds it dear?

These plans I leave, the wind is clear.

As incense swirls, so memories rise,

And drift beyond the song's own guise.

My gaze, too late, to ears now turns,

Where echoes land, where passion burns.

My love, you show my twisted ways,
First turned to last, in hazy maze.
Each life a journey, vast and lone,
No phantom mate, to walk on stone.

We meet by chance, and one become,
Beyond all praise, the silent hum.
Inscribe your mark, on waves unseen,
You, essence deep, of what has been.

I praise you, oh, the endless way,
Where light and dark forever play.

UNVEILING TRUE LOVE

Bonds of false affection, love's true nature fades,
A ritualistic dance, where passion softly bleeds.
In freedom's name, ego's desires unfettered roam,
Our true nature unguarded, they fill with gloom.

Love, sacrifice, and mercy, gifts granted so free,
Not mere desires to covet, but virtues born to be.
Freedom's vibrant essence, a character defined,
Our birth right the unwritten code of humankind

As love's essence withers and turn to stone,
Carved in rigid postures, where feelings flown.
Rock-solid accolades, a hollow, empty praise,
Bring not life's vibrancy, but shadows in a haze.

Life's essence, a perennial river, flowing deep,
I fail to grasp its secrets, lessons I cannot keep.
Painless suffocation, a heart with love imbued,
Seeking your breath, my love be renewed

A messenger of love, I pray you make me so,
A reflection of your grace, a love all may know.
A nectar sweet, your perfection's gentle touch,
Endless seeking for love means so much.

Wisdom diminished and sullied by desire,
Cleans me of the dross of this false attire,
Oh! you, whose love knows no bounds,
Master of the multiverse, love forever resounds.

WHAT MAKES YOU SAME –
FROM CRADLE TO GRAVE

What makes you same, from cradle to grave,
As life's grand tapestry, your story weaves,
Many years pass and moments gently fade,
Your essence remains, a soul that believes

From the cradle, your innocence pure and bright,
With eyes that gleam like stars in endless night,
A heart so tender, free from worldly plight,
Your laughter and your wonder, a guiding light.

Through childhood's joys, you learn and grow,
The world unfolds, its wonders to bestow,
Your dreams take root, like seeds they sow,
The essence of your spirit begins to show.

As youth beckons, your passions brightly burn,
With every lesson learned, each twist and turn,
You seek your place, your purpose, and discern,
The fires of ambition fiercely within you churn.

Adulthood comes with burdens and with grace,
You find your stride, your unique life's pace,
With each new challenge, you'll find your place,
As the same core values you still embrace.

In later years, when wisdom's whispers near,
You've weathered storms, both joy and fear,
Same heart beats, though time may pass,
Your love and laughter, to all, will surpass.

From cradle to grave, your spirit stands the test,
Enduring, evolving, through each life's bequest,
The same core self within your boundless chest,
A timeless soul, in each moment, blessed.

WHISPERS OF AZURE PASSION

In realms where sky meets the earth's attire,
Blue is the color of a whispered fire.
Desire dances in the azure expanse,
Nature and cosmos share a cosmic dance.

Beneath the canopy, a tranquil sea,
Reflections of longing, profound and free.
The cerulean canvas, a celestial lyre,
Where dreams unfold in hues of desire.

Above, the stars in their cosmic choir,
Painting constellations with passion's fire.
Blue galaxies swirl in a cosmic mire,
A celestial waltz, a dance entire.

Mountains echo the desire to aspire,
Their peaks kissed by the sapphire spire.
Rivers weave through landscapes entire,
Carrying tales of passion in liquid attire.

Barnabas Tiburtius § 185

In meadows where wildflowers conspire,
Petals unfurl in a dance of desire.
Blue butterflies flutter, their wings inspire,
A symphony of color, nature's attire.

As day surrenders to night's attire,
Moonlight bathes in a silver lyre.
The cosmos whispers, stoking desire,
A celestial ballad, ever higher.

In the quiet of twilight, when stars retire,
Blue lingers on, the soul's burning pyre.
Nature and cosmos, entwined entire,
In the cosmic embrace of desire.

WHISPERS OF LIGHT – ECHOES OF GRACE

Unfurling landscapes, heart alight,
A traveller's joy, a wondrous sight.
No garb nor dust, nor hunger's bite,
Just gazing deep, with keenest sight.

Companion dear, on cosmic quest,
Through your eyes, life's essence blessed.
A pause, a doubt, "Who am I, then?"
Lost in applause, a fleeting sin.

Screams and tears, a home's loud fray,
Now like a child, I long to stray.
To mother's touch, a solace deep,
In her kind eyes, where dreams can sleep.

Footsteps traced, a journey past,
Seeking solace, memories cast.
In fleeting light, my spirit wanes,
Father's voice, a guiding cane.

"Live!" it calls, with love's decree,
A gift of grace, for all to see.
Oh, dawn's first light, your wisdom's flame,
I sing your praise, forever name.

Though form may change, and meaning bend,
This verse's heart, its message sends:
With open eyes and spirit free,
Find joy, dear friend, in all you see.

WHISPERS OF REDEMPTION

Life's tapestry, we all play part.
Dreams, hopes journey, where tales start.
Heart's effort, gift to fate we lend.
Someday, a union with cosmos we end.

Everything repays, we're told.
Each heart's whisper, love held tight.
Not as wished, or once believed.
Fate's twists relieve our souls.

Heartache, tears, vast disappointments.
Threads in tapestry, past has sown.
What redeems pain, makes spirits soar?
Hope's soil where dreams take root.

Leaves of Grass, Whitman's words unfold.
Life's truth told, a testament.
Anguish heart, in verse found lease.
Heartbreak transformed, a masterpiece.

Parentheses hid his wisdom's keep.
Life's tide relentless, lesson deep.
Dream's dissolution, heartache sore.
Fertile soil where new dreams soar.

Like grass leaves, we rise and fall.
Through joy, heartbreak, in love's call.
Life's melody, in high and low.
Echoes' symphony, stories flow.

Cherish journey, with twists and turns.
New light burns in broken learns.
Embrace truth Whitman's art knew.
Heart beats in life's transform new.

WHISPERS OF THE HEART – A POEM IN BLOOM

A gentle touch, a bud's caress,

No startle brings, but tender stress.

A sweetness blooms, unseen, unknown,

Softens the heart, a life unblown.

The Muse arrives, a sacred guest,

Outside the door, it puts me to the test.

My mind, it wavers, cries in vain,

"Is this the spark, the whispered strain?"

My poetry, a wild, free verse,

No definition can rehearse.

Love, hate, or sorrow, dark or bright,

It dances free in day and night.

With regal gaze, it scans the scene,
Ensures all's well, serene, pristine.
Then, like a dancer, light and strong,
It claims its throne, where it belongs.

No earthly food my verse can bring,
Nor fame's applause with empty ring.
What need of honour, fleeting praise?
In its deep eyes, I find my gaze.

The light too fierce, I blink and see,
A message whispered, meant for me.
Oh, fountain of grace, your love unbound,
In poetry's flow, it's richly found.

Oh, cloud of love, that overflows,
With gentle strength, where kindness grows.
Your boundless gift, it pours and stays,
A mother's love that lights my days.

Devotion's call, a whispered plea,
The greatest good, to bend my knee.
Oh, wonder praised, forever known,
A heart's sweet song, a seed now sown.

WHISPERS OF THE WILD

Set sail upon the Alaskan sound,
Where silent waters speak,
The boat's soft hum, echoing rebound,
Through peaks snow-covered, sleek.

Majestic cliffs on either side,
Their crowns in powdered white,
Stand guard as gods, timeless guides,
In the golden morning light.

Through lush green forests, dense and pure,
With whispers of the wild,
Where nature's secrets rest assured,
In the heart of earth's deep child.

Eagles soar with regal grace,
Above the tranquil sea,
Reflected in the water's face,
A dance uninhabited, and free.

The air is crisp, the breeze is cold,
Yet warmth in awe is found,
In beauty vast and tales untold,
Within this sacred sound.

As daylight fades and stars ascend,
The twilight soft hues painted mild,
On this journey's wondrous end,
My soul radiates love undefiled

YEARNING IN STILLNESS

In hushed repose, where life's loud clamor sleeps,
My ears yearn for the whisper of your tread,
A balm that soothes, a comfort that it keeps.

The world's bright show, a whirlwind in my head,
I close my eyes, and bid these sights depart,
To glimpse the inner light within your heart.

They say that taste, of senses holds the crown,
But on your sweetness, all my taste buds wait,
For no delight can ever be quite renown,
The nectar of your love, divine and great.

Let fleeting scents, so potent and so false,
Not drown me in their haze, a fleeting bloom,
But let me breathe the fragrance, a sweet waltz,
Your essence, love, that fills and doth consume.

Oh, my beloved, wellspring of my days,
The foundation where my love finds form,
I cast aside the touch of others' ways,
To hold you close, safe from the coming storm.

My every word, my thought, my very breath,
Without your mark, they have no life to claim,
A silent prayer, a yearning deep as death,
An offering to you, my heart's own flame.

Truth's dark maze, shadows weave spell.
Hold me, guide, lest I lose way.
Wisdom's path unfolds, gentle swell.
Mother's voice praised, words that stay.